MOVING THE M

Julian Stray

THE *MOBILE* POST OFFICE

PUBLIC TELEPHONES
LOCAL & TRUNK SERVICES

GPO

THE BRITISH POSTAL MUSEUM & ARCHIVE

Published by
The British Postal Museum & Archive
Freeling House
Phoenix Place
LONDON
WCIX 0DL

Text © The British Postal Museum & Archive 2006

ISBN 10: 0-9553569-0-3
ISBN 13: 978-0-9553569-0-2

Designed by Jeff Teader, JVT Design, London

Manufactured in the EU by L.P.P.S.Ltd, Wellingborough,
Northants NN8 3PJ

CONTENTS

List of Illustrations   v

Introduction   I

By Horse...   5

The Post Boy   5
The Mail Coach
Horse-Drawn Vans   I0

By Cycle...   I7

Two, three or five wheels?   I7
Contemporary use   2I

By Motorcycle...   23

Combinations and Tri-cars   23
Solo machines   26
Mopeds   28

By Motor...   33

Early Choices: Steam, Electric & Oil Drives   33
A first purchase: 'Maudslay No. I'   37
Vehicles during World War I   38
The Post Office moves towards owning its own fleet   4I
Ford & Morris Vehicles   44
Vehicles during World War II   47
Getting the Right Size & the Right Engines   48
Size of the fleet   52
Cutting down on pollution   53

By Specialised Vehicles...   57

Postbus   58
The Mobile Post Office   62
Royal Air Mail Service   65
Electric Vehicles   68

Appendix I   74

Sources & Credits   77

Further Information   79

Note:
Post Office vehicles have traditionally been rated by their carrying capacity.
Conversions for these and some other measurements that appear in the text
are as follows:

cu ft	=cubic foot (ft3)	=1728 in3	=0.0283 m3
1 cwt	=1 hundredweight	=112 pound (lb)	=50.802 kg
1 pound (lb)	=16 ounce (oz)	=0.4536 kg	
1 ton	=20 cwt	=1.016 tonne (t)	=1000 kg
1 mile	=1760 yard (yd)	=1.6093 km	

LIST OF ILLUSTRATIONS

Caution to Postboys	1
Brighton Parcel Mail Coach, 1 June 1905	2
Milnes Daimler parcel van at Brighton, 1905	4
Morris vans and BSA motorcycle combinations	4
Hand carts, parcel delivery	4
Aboyne Postbus. Image used in Post Office booklet *Take a Letter* in 1990	4
Post boy, c1800	5
Stamp artwork: The original Bath Mail Coach of 1784	6
Stamp artwork: An Attack on the Exeter Mail in 1816	6
Stamp artwork: The Holyhead & Liverpool Mails 1828	6
Stamp artwork: The Edinburgh Mail snowbound in 1831	6
Stamp artwork: The Norwich Mail in a Thunder Storm 1837	6
Time bill, 1840	7
Notice advertising the evening departures from The Swan with Two Necks, Pre 1846	9
'Last of the Mail Coach Guards' by H E Brown c1890	10
Mc Namara's Kennington stables	12
Last horse-drawn mail van	14
Post Office specification for a single-horse van for the Parcels Post	15
Unloading mailbags from horse drawn carts at London Office Loading Bay	15
Parcel post van and a twin-driven cycle parcel post carrier. 1887	15
Shenley postmen with bicycle and mail cart outside the local postman's shelter, 1912	16
Penny Post Jubilee, 1890	16
Centre-cycles, Horsham, 1882	17
Advertisement from The Postman's Gazette, 26 March 1898	18

Postman with tricycle and basket carrier 1934 19

Postman with a standard design delivery bicycle on a
suburban delivery route, 1938 20

The Mailstar delivery bicycle, Southall, London
2000 – 2002 21

Postmen with bicycles at the start of their rounds, c1920 22

Postwoman with a step-through bicycle, 1949 22

Postwomen with bicycles, Barnet, c1915 22

Stamp booklet, 1993 23

First motorised mail at Sittingbourne, c1902 23

First rural post car Sittingbourne, Kent, 1910 24

Tri-car at Oakham Post Office, c1915 25

Rural motor-tricycle at Clapham Post Office, c1905 25

Post Office messengers on BSA motorcycles, 1933 27

Group of Telegraph Messengers on BSA motorcycles
at Ealing, c1934 27

Expresspost service, 1981 29

Honda Quad-bike, January 2002 30

Postman and BSA solo motorcycle on postal delivery
work near Tavistock, 1929 31

Motorcycle combination, 1932 31

GPO poster to advertise the Telegram Service by
Pat Keely, 1950 32

Daimler motor van, 1898 36

Maudslay Stores 'No.1' 37

Morris Z van with wartime adaptations 39

Artwork for 1985 stamp issue 46

Morris Minor on front cover of leaflet 'News-information',
October 1963 46

Morris Z Type during World War II 47

Scammell 'Mechanical Horse', Aberdeen, 1942-3 47

Royal Mail Morris 'Z type' vans outside Yeading
repair and paint shop, c1950   48

Photograph from *A look at Royal Mail's vehicle fleet*
produced in 1993   50

Reliant three-wheeled van   51

Refuelling with Liquified Petroleum Gas (LPG)
at Mount Pleasant, London, 2005   54

First Post Office vehicle fleet prior to World War I   55

Motor Transport Workshop, Studd Street, London   55

Morris Commercial. 105 cubic feet capacity, 1934   55

Iveco Ford. Motor Transport Service Bulletin specifying
vehicle livery, December 1987   55

Mail vans gathered in the yard at King Edward Building,
London, 1931   56

Parcelforce Worldwide van, 2006   56

Post Office notice, 1954

Poster advertising the *First Royal Mail Post Bus in Kent*   58

Postbus Ticket issued 17 September 1974   59

Inauguration of the Post Bus service, Llanidloes, Wales,
20 February 1967   59

Land Rovers   60

Postbus and driver, Sittingbourne, Kent, 2006   61

Vauxhall Brava Postbus (4x4)   61

Cover of advertising booklet for new Mobile Post Office
service, 1937   63

Mobile Post Office 'GPO 2' alongside the cruise-liner
Queen Elizabeth   62

Registered envelope serviced at the Mobile Post Office,
April 7-10 1937   62

Design brief for 'mega-unit' Mobile Post Office
introduced in the 1980s   64

Mobile Post Office, 2006   65

New Mobile Post Offices awaiting transfer to their regions   65

Morris Air Mail Van, 1930-38   65

Streamlined airmail car at Liverpool aerodrome, 1935   66

Morris airmail van, Croydon Airport, 1933   66

Air Mail leaflet, 1930-38   67

Royal Mail airmail delivery van, Croydon   67

Electricars' tow-truck   68

Daimler electric mail van, 1899   68

Electromobile battery powered postal vans at Leeds, 1928   69

Stamp booklet, 1994   69

Pedestrian controlled Electric Delivery Truck,
Battersea, 1954   70

Bradshaw delivery van, Oxford, 2006   72

Streamlined Airmail van, Liverpool   72

Mobile Post Office at outdoor event in 1930s   72

Mobile Post Office, Edinburgh   73

Amphibious vehicle   73

Stamp booklet, 1994   73

INTRODUCTION

The task of collecting, transporting and delivering the mail has become steadily more complex over the years as the volumes of mail increase, and the delivery destinations become evermore widespread. The post was opened up under Charles I in 1635, when it first became possible for the general public to send a letter through a postal system.

Volumes of mail carried boomed, resulting in a need for increased efficiency in road transport. The system of boys riding in relay carrying messages on horseback gave way to a swift and efficient mail coach service. This in turn saw a move toward transport on the newly emerging railways.

CAUTION to POST-BOYS.

BY the Act of 5th of Geo. III. If any Poft-Boy, or Rider, having taken any of His Majefty's Mails, or Bags of Letters, under his Care, to convey to the next Poft Town or Stage, fhall fuffer any other Perfon (except a Guard) to ride on the Horfe or Carriage, or fhall Loiter on the Road, and wilfully mifpend his Time, fo as to retard the Arrival of the faid Mails, or Bags of Letters, at the next Poft Town or Stage.—Every fuch Offender fhall, on Conviction before One Juftice, be committed to the Houfe of Correction, and confined to hard Labour for one Month. All Poft-Boys and Riders are therefore defired to take Notice of this, and are hereby cautioned not to fail in the regular Performance of their Duty, otherwife they will moft affuredly be punifhed as the Law directs. And it is hoped and requefted, for the Benefit of public Correfpondence, that all Perfons, who may obferve any Poft-Boy or Rider, offending as aforefaid, will give immediate Notice to — *Johnson Williams* Surveyor of the General Poft-Office, at (*About* 1792)

Caution to Post boys
Surveyor's caution to Post Boys not to fail in their regular performance of their duty, circa 1792.
BPMA P8078

In 1840, Rowland Hill's visionary scheme for a Uniform Penny Post saw the mail service fall within the means of a far greater proportion of the general population. It was not until 1897, as a move to celebrate Queen Victoria's Diamond Jubilee, that delivery to all addresses in the United Kingdom became standard.

Toward the end of the 19th century, in addition to a rail network, the Post Office continued to rely predominantly on contractors to fulfil its road transport operations. To supplement the traditional horse-drawn vehicles, there were new forms of transport on the horizon, however the Post Office continued to rely on the contractor to bear the costs and associated risks of any newly emerging technology.

Brighton Parcel Mail coach, 1 June 1905
The last horse drawn service between London and Brighton was replaced by a motorised van the following day. Thomas Tilling, mail contractors, supplied both driver and van.
BPMA P.3564

Milnes Daimler parcel van at Brighton, 1905
Operated by Thomas Tilling under contract to the Post Office. Vehicle ran between London and Brighton, it replaced the previous horse-drawn service on
2 June 1905
BPMA P.3565

Using the Royal Mail Archive for original research reveals important contemporary commentary. Not only on developments in road transport from officials and others working for the Post Office, but also those of contractors working with the organisation. Examining these advances provides a fascinating insight into a popular aspect of postal history, as well as the history of road transport from horses, through cycles and motorcycles, to motor vehicles.

It is often the initial development of any emergent form of transport that is of particular interest, and it is on this that the following text concentrates. The Post Office fleet has, at times, been a bewilderingly diverse collection of vehicles. Detailed records of the types and numbers of vehicles in the fleet in specific years are of interest, especially when compared to the vast and complex organisation that Royal Mail Group plc is today.

The provision of an efficient road transport network is not the end of the story. This publication also touches on less well known developments. These vary from combining mail transport with the provision of a public transport system to taking counter services out onto the road, and the story continues. These and some other (occasionally short-lived) developments are covered here.

The speedy and efficient movement of mails is the common facet to the history of Royal Mail's modern fleet deserves a closer inspection. Its vehicles have helped to maintain that most basic of requirements: our need to communicate.

Post Office or Royal Mail?
It can be confusing to see both 'Royal Mail' and 'Post Office' used together in any account of its history. It might be helpful to remember while reading this text, that the former is *almost invariably* referring to the 'letters' function, while 'Post Office' *usually* refers to the larger parent company that encompassed

other aspects of the business from counters service to telephones. In the 1930s a motorcycle sporting 'GPO' (General Post Office) on its leg shields could pass a van emblazoned with the 'Royal Mail' brand going one way, and a 'Post Office Telephones' van going the other. To make matters more complex, things change. Today the business is comprised of Royal Mail, Post Office™ and Parcelforce Worldwide which operate as part of Royal Mail Group plc, and the telephones aspect of the business is now run by BT Group plc.

Top to bottom:

i) Morris vans and BSA motorcycle combinations
BPMA

ii) Hand carts, parcel delivery
Hand Carts. The introduction of the Parcels Post in 1883 and moves in 1897 toward a delivery to all addresses in the United Kingdom resulted in a dramatic increase in the volume of mail carried. Letter Carriers now no longer carried letters, as a result, they were given a new title, henceforth they were known as 'Postmen'
BPMA

iii) Aboyne Postbus. Image used in Post Office booklet 'Take a Letter' in 1990.
BPMA

The Post Boy

The Royal Mail first made use of horses for the transport of messages when it was precisely that, a service created to carry the King's despatches. The court of Henry III used royal messengers in the 13th century, and over the following three hundred years an efficient system of riders travelling in relay between 'Posts' or stages was created. Horses were kept solely for use on this service, and regular lines of communication were established on major routes such as those to Scotland or to Dover for mainland Europe.

Each relay, or 'Post', was some 20 miles in length, being the distance a horse could comfortably travel at speed before needing to be replaced. Post Boys had to blow their horn at least every four miles to warn approaching travellers to make way for the Royal Mail. A speed of seven miles per hour was generally maintained, but adverse weather in winter meant that this could be reduced to five miles per hour.

Post boy circa 1800
BPMA P8910 folder 21

5

Regulations were drawn up in 1574 stipulating that each 'Post Master' was to have at least three horses constantly available for use. When he heard the sound of the rider's post horn signifying the imminent arrival of a packet of mail, he was to prepare his own Post Boy for despatch within 15 minutes for the next stage of the mail's journey.

Top to bottom:

i) The original Bath Mail Coach, 1784

ii) An attack on the Exeter Mail, 1816

iii) The Norwich Mail in a thunder storm, 1837

iv) The Holyhead & Liverpool Mails, 1828

v) The Edinburgh Mail snowbound 1831
Artwork for the set of five stamps issued in July 1984 to commemorate the bicentenary of the first mail coach run, Bath and Bristol to London. *BPMA Philatelic collection*

THE *Original* BATH Mail Coach *of 1784*

AN *Attack on the* EXETER Mail *in 1816*

THE HOLYHEAD & LIVERPOOL Mails *1828*

THE EDINBURGH Mail *Snowbound in 1831*

THE NORWICH Mail *in a Thunder Storm 1827*

The Mail Coach

The mail coach was the brainchild of John Palmer. When proposing his new scheme to the Post Office, Palmer had expressed his contempt for the existing system of Post Boys in a forthright style:

"The Post, at present, instead of being the swiftest, is almost the slowest, conveyance in the country; and though, from the great improvement in our roads, other carriers have proportionally mended their speed, the post is as slow as ever. It is likewise very unsafe as the frequent robberies of it testify…the mails are generally entrusted to some idle boy, without character, mounted on a worn-out hack, and who, so far from being able to defend himself or escape from a robber, is much more likely to be in league with him"
John Palmer, Theatre Manager and Entrepreneur

Dangers encountered by the Post Boys on the road meant that it could be difficult to recruit new 'Boys' to the position. Palmer was therefore permitted to introduce his new system which required swift changes of teams of horses every 10 miles, thereby allowing a high average speed to be maintained by the coaches. A record time of 16 hours between London and Bristol was attained on the very first journey.

The first mail coach ran between Bristol and London via Bath on 2 August 1784. The service was recorded in the local newspaper:

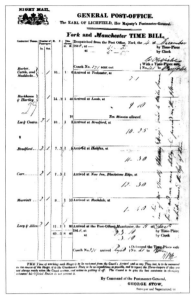

Time bill, 1840
Used on the York and Manchester route, and records the arrival times of the mail coach at the appointed stages where horses were changed. This bill also records the death of a horse on the journey and the subsequent delay.
4 December 1840
BPMA

"Our Mail Diligence still continues its course with the same steadiness and punctuality; yesterday its coachman and guard made their first appearance in royal livery, and cut a most superior figure."
Bath Chronicle, 16 September 1784

Heavily armed with a blunderbuss and a brace of pistols the guard was entrusted to ensure the safe conduct of the mails. The mail guard was the only Post Office employee on the coach. In 1786, a highwayman attempted to hold up the mails and was shot dead on the spot, sending out a clear message to other would-be highwaymen. No further attempts were ever made on the mail coaches.

In common with the Post Boys, the mail guard carried a horn with which he alerted other road users and toll gatekeepers. He also warned coaching inns of his imminent arrival allowing them time to get fresh horses prepared and ready. Teams of horses varied from two to six depending on the route and even blind horses could be included within a team.

Mail coach livery was very impressive. The upper half of the coach body was black, the bottom half and doors were maroon and the wheels were red. The Royal Arms and cipher were applied to the coach sides and each coach carried the words 'Royal Mail' and the names of the route termini. Coaches bore the four principal stars of the orders of knighthood; these were the Garter, the Bath, the Thistle and St. Patrick.

By the spring of 1785, mail coaches from London were travelling to Norwich, Liverpool and Leeds. By the end of the year they were also serving Dover, Portsmouth, Poole, Exeter, Gloucester, Worcester, Holyhead and Carlisle. The following year, the 400 or so miles to Edinburgh were being covered in 60 hours. In addition to London-based coaches, services also commenced between provincial post towns, with over 80 different routes being established. However, the condition of the roads in some parts of the country proved too perilous for these services. In 1808, when the Post Office attempted to run a mail coach between Shrewsbury and Holyhead three horses suffered broken legs in one week.

The original mail coaches were poorly prepared for their role and had constructional defects; they were cheaply made and could not stand up to the rigours of the road. Palmer decided to use the 'Patent Coach' of the London builder John Besant. Following Besant's death in 1791 Besant's partner, John Vidler, continued to supply mail coaches to the Post Office for over 40 years.

Figures involved with running mail coaches routes were considerable. In 'The Story of the Road' (1836), Professor Gregory records that a William Chaplin owned 3,000 coaches and 150,000 horses. He employed 30,000 drivers, guards and ostlers, and was contracted to provide 27 mail coaches, which ran out of London nightly.

Coaches carried a maximum of four passengers at first, all of whom had to sit inside. After a few years, an additional two passengers were permitted to travel outside, but only if they sat at the front. The guard remained a solitary figure at the rear. The sight of all the mail coaches leaving the General Post Office in St Martin's-le-Grand, London was considered such a spectacle that crowds of people would gather in the evening to observe it.

Notice advertising the evening departures of Royal Mail coaches from one of the main London posting inns, The Swan with Two Necks, Lad Lane. Pre 1846. *BPMA ref: 2005.81/14. Acquired with the assistance of the V & A Purchase Fund*

The mail coach was the speediest road service in the country and brought with it not only the mail, but also news of events far removed from the towns and villages that it passed through. In 1849, Thomas De Quincey wrote in 'The English Mail-Coach' that:

"The mail-coach it was that distributed over the face of the land, like the opening of apocalyptic vials, the heart-shaking news of Trafalgar, of Salamanca, of Vittoria, of Waterloo... The mail-coach, as the national organ for publishing these mighty events, thus diffusively influential, became itself a spiritualised and glorified object to an impassioned heart."

The last London-based mail coach, between London and Norwich, via Newmarket, ran in April 1846. For all the increased speed that the mail coaches provided, they could not match that of the emerging railway system. As ever, quick to engage with new technology, the Post Office had begun experiments with the railways, although they continued to use horses to deliver the mail for a further hundred years after the demise of the last mail coach.

Mails were first carried by rail on the new Liverpool and
Manchester Railway in 1830. Eight years later, on 22 May,
the mail coaches for Holyhead, Manchester, Liverpool and
Carlisle were carried on the rail trucks of the Euston-
Birmingham Railway. Many of the mail guards who had
previously accompanied the mail coaches transferred to the
railways. Initially, they continued to sit above the carriages as they

had on the road. In 1837 after a
series of complaints the provision
of... '*shades for the eyes...*' was
made for mail guards to protect
them from '... *the wind and
cinders, or rather sparks, from the
chimney of the steam engine*'.
Within a few years however, they
were accompanying the mails
within the train carriages.

'Last of the Mail
Coach Guards' by
HE Brown. Circa
1890
Portrait of Moses
Nobbs in uniform,
painted some 40
years after mail
coaches stopped.
BPMA

Not all coachmen viewed the
demise of the mail coaches as a
progressive move:

"*Them as 'ave seen coaches afore rails came into fashion 'ave seen
something worth rememberin'! Them was 'appy days for old England,
afore reform and rails turned everything upside down.*"
Recollections of a coachman, *St Martin's-le-Grand Magazine*

Horse-Drawn Vans

"*...from 15 to 16 hands, about 10cwt, clean limbed trotters,
rising five...*"
Post Office specification for the provision of horses

In September 1829, four 'accelerator carriages' were introduced
in London to convey letter carriers from the GPO, St. Martin's-
le-Grand, to the start of their delivery. Designed so that the men
could step off of the vehicle while it was still moving, each

accelerator could carry 12 or so men. In 1857, Rowland Hill's plan (approved the previous year) that divided London into 10 postal districts came into operation. From this date, because the men were now based locally at the new District Offices, there was no longer the need to carry letter carriers to the outlying districts.

The emergence of the railways provided exactly what was required by the Post Office: a regular, efficient transport of mails. Notwithstanding the occasional accident or delay, rail services continued to improve in reliability. Nonetheless, for conveyance of the mails between provincial towns and transfer to and from the railway stations, the effective acceleration of an ever increasing volume of mail could still only be achieved by means of an efficient road service.

The Post Office preferred not to own its own horse-drawn mail van service. Instead the individual routes were contracted out with successful applicants providing vans to a specified design. The Post Office had considered maintaining its own livery (it was even suggested that it could do so by taking over the horses from any of the contractors dispensed with) but preferred to remain using contractors. The use of animals was not confined just to horses. On occasion donkeys have been drawn into service on rural deliveries by cart, but this was exceptional.

> "I am one of the few [mail van drivers] to have had to tackle a load of snakes. They must have escaped from a bag of foreign mail that I picked up at the docks…when I reached the post office the van was crawling with them. I was glad to remember the rule that post officials only must unload"
> Memories of a Mail Driver, H. Styles, The Post, 27 February 1932

Contractors also supplied the drivers who were duly provided with Post Office uniforms. Work could be frenetic: drivers would commence the day with a large van on a morning round, do a midday run with a delivery van and finish off with a light one-horse letter cart. Despite their hard work, one of the principal London contractors, Bolton and Allen, was less than generous with their observations on the character of their drivers:

"As a rule drivers are not a well-educated class, most of them take more to drink than is good for them, bringing on bad temper, recklessness, sleep and so on...it is a common experience to find a man who would as soon run over one as pull a rein"
Horse-drawn mail vans, St Martin's-le-Grand, July 1930

Charles Dickens also recorded this hazard to the unwary road user in his novel 'Little Dorrit'. One of the characters, Clenman, observes someone being carried from an accident and receives the following answer when he questions a man in the street:

'They ought to be prosecuted and fined, them Mails. They come a racing out of Lad Lane and Wood Street at twelve or fourteen mile an hour, them Mails do. The only wonder is, that people ain't killed oftener by them Mails"

Much of the hazard can be attributed to the fact that until 1889 mail vans did not carry any lights at night until they were 'requested' to do so by the Postmaster General in December 1888. This is all the more unusual considering that the mail coaches some 50 years previously had been considered the best-lit vehicles on the road.

McNamara's
Kennington stables
One of the
principal London
mail contractors
BPMA

Contracted services increased further following the introduction of the Parcels Post in 1883. The railways took 55% of the receipts for all parcels carried by rail, which loss of income encouraged the Post Office to reintroduce a horse-drawn road service in 1887. By this means it was able to retain 100% of the profits from any parcels carried by road as routes were contracted out for a fixed fee for the route. The Post Office was now able to accept the most competitive tender, which was not the case on the railways.

The decline in the number of horses in the service of the London mail contractors between 1908 and 1912

Contractor	Number of horses employed	
	1908	**1912**
Mc Namara	760	490
J. Allen	500	500
Birch Bros.	400	330
Webster	325	-
Total	**1985**	**1320**
Tilling	By 1908, these two contractors were	
Leyland	only running motor services in London	

Prior to 1919, nearly all of the road mail services were in the hands of contractors, and it was the high cost demanded for these services that encouraged the Post Office to introduce its own motor vehicle fleet. By 1930, the Post Office ran 179 of the 766 motor services and 10 of the 74 horse services themselves.

World War II and the accompanying petrol rationing encouraged the retention of a horse-drawn service longer than it might have survived otherwise, and it was not until 1949 that the last horse-drawn mail van left King Edward Building post office in the heart of London.

Last horse-drawn
mail van
Pulled by 'Peter',
leaving the East
Central District
Office, London, 24
September 1949.
BPMA ref: P4295

The use of horses has continued to some extent though. Just
occasionally the lone postman or woman, when faced with the
prospect of crossing moors or flooded fields, has returned to
that oldest form of mail transportation. Just as their postal
predecessors had relied on equine surefootedness, so too has the
modern mail service occasionally looked to the reliability of the
horse to permit a daily delivery of letters to continue.

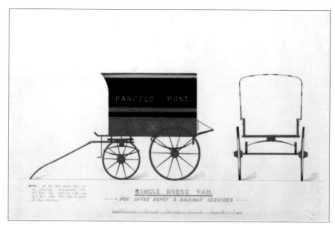

Post Office specification for a single-horse van for the Parcels Post service inter depot and on railway services, 1883.
BPMA POST 25

Unloading mailbags from horse drawn carts at London Office Loading Bay Contractor's drivers were not permitted to handle the mail themselves,
BPMA

Parcel post van and a twin-driven cycle parcel post carrier, 1887.
BPMA ref: P5945

Shenley postmen with bicycle and mail cart outside the local postman's shelter, 1912.
BPMA ref: P9551

Penny Post Jubilee, 1890
A grand procession at Guildhall, London of the various types of Royal Mail vehicles in use. This photograph shows one of the light single-horse mailcarts preparing for the parade.

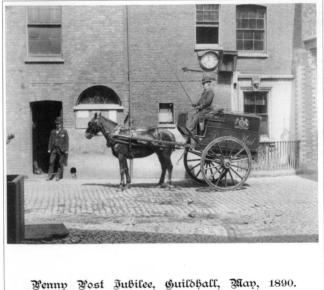

Penny Post Jubilee, Guildhall, May, 1890.

Two, three or five wheels?

The Post Office first made use of tricycles for the delivery of mail during 1880 in Coventry, a town that was to supply a considerable number of bicycles and motorised vehicles to the Post Office in the years to follow.

Two years later in 1882, trials were held with pentacycles in the Horsham district in Sussex. These five-wheeled machines, also known as Centre Cycles or colloquially as 'Hen and Chickens', were regarded favourably in some quarters. Overall, however, the experiment was deemed a failure, and they never entered wider service.

Centre-cycles, Horsham, 1882

In 1897, the radius for free delivery of telegrams was increased from one to three miles. In addition, all letters were as far as possible to be delivered at least once a day. The Post Office Engineer-in-Chief's Office was instructed to purchase 100 bicycles for telegram messengers and postmen. These were purchased by the Controller of Telegraph Stores from the Quadrant Cycle Co. A standard bicycle specification had been

Advertisement from The Postman's Gazette encouraging postmen to buy cycles for use at work. 26 March 1898. BPMA POST 115

adopted at this time but it was withdrawn as a matter of policy by the Postmaster General, Sir Austen Chamberlain, in 1902 when the purchase of trade pattern bicycles was ordered.

The earlier standard design had drawn considerable praise, and it was reported that:

"...the bulk of these machines has been built by one Coventry and one Birmingham firm to the Departments own specification, and as the bicycles so admirably stand the enormous wear and tear they are called upon to undergo in all weathers...the knowledge gained should prove of immense value in the designing of suitable machines for military purposes."
Bicycling News, 1900

The design proved so popular that manufacturers would frequently advertise their products available to the general public as the 'G.P.O. model'.

In some rural areas postmen provided their own cycles and the Post Office paid a weekly allowance towards their maintenance. However, the provision of official machines continued and by 1909, over 5,000 postmen had been provided with bicycles, carrier-cycles and bicycles with trailing carts. There were also 750 Post Office linesmen using cycles to help them maintain the telegraph lines that crossed the country. In addition a number of supervising and inspecting officers made use of cycles.

Bicycle trailers were supplied by companies that included Mills & Fulford, The Oxford Automobile Agency, W.P. Heighton Ltd. and the Abingdon Works Ltd. At first they were fitted with a basket for storing mails, although one manufacturer fitted a box instead. In keeping with the red pillar boxes and mail vans, bicycles were usually coated with red enamel, although those used by Inspecting and Supervising Officers were enamelled black. Bicycles used for telegraph duties and ridden by boys had a fixed driving wheel, whilst those ridden by men on Post Office duty were fitted with free wheels and two brakes.

The use of tricycles diminished around the end of the 19th century as loads increased together with the strain on the rider. There was also a recommendation to replace the tricycle posts. In 1914 Post Office porters were used on 180 tricycle services in London but even then the vehicles were thought out of date. Had light motor vehicles been available then, they would have been used instead.

Postman with tricycle and basket carrier, 1934.
BPMA ref: POST1 18/127

"Horse-drawn vehicles and tricycle carriers are antiquated and the latter impose considerable hardship on the men especially in severe weather and I should like to see them replaced by motor vehicles wherever possible"
BPMA, POST 30/7604, 3 May 1919

The load-carrying capacity and maximum distance to which a cycle-mounted post could operate actually compared quite favourably with that attainable by other means. The table below shows the figures that applied in 1927.

	Foot	Horse or horse and cart	Cycle	Solo Motorcycle	Combination Motorcycle	Light van	Heavy van
Average speed (mph)	3	4-8	6	15	15	15	12
Maximum Distance (miles)	18	21	26-28	70	65	75	75
Load capacity	35 lb	limit of cart capacity	50 lb	70 lb	168 lb – 280 lb	5 cwt – 8 cwt (560 – 896 lb)	12 cwt – 25 cwt (1344 – 2800 lb)

The overall number of official bicycles and tricycles employed on postal services in town and rural districts had increased to 20,000 by 1927. An allowance of one shilling per week was paid to Postmen for carrying out cleaning and repairs outside official hours. By 1933, some 200 million miles were being covered each year by the cycle posts.

Postman with a standard design delivery bicycle on a suburban delivery route. 1938.
BPMA ref: P2127

A number of manufacturers have provided cycles for the Post Office over the years, amongst them are Elswick, James and Townsend. Another manufacturer, Pashley, became the main supplier in 1977. The design of the bicycle itself used for delivering the mail remained virtually unaltered between 1929 and 1992, a total of 63 years. In 1992, the number of cycles being used had risen to 35,000 for mail delivery.

Contemporary use

Experiments have continued with less conventional types of cycle. During 1997 Royal Mail carried out a short-term study in Bridgwater, Somerset with the four-wheeled, feet-forward Brox cycle. As well as being efficient, it was also discovered that the depreciation of such a top of the range cycle was far less than that of a postal van. Despite the additional cost of fuel for a van and cheaper maintenance for the cycle the trial was not extended further.

At the beginning of the 21st century, two new bicycles manufactured by Pashley were introduced to the fleet. 'Mailstar' and 'Millennium' were phased in as part of a seven-year replacement policy adopted by the business.

Royal Mail has the largest fleet of bicycles in the UK, totalling 36,000 in 2006. In keeping with other modes of transport, safety has become a prime concern. Reflective clothing and cycle helmets are now provided for the riders. The front carrier has been replaced with a deep tray mounted to avoid the danger of loose straps being entangled in the front wheel. Rear panniers are also

The Mailstar delivery bicycle, Southall, London. First manufactured between 2000-2002 for Royal Mail by Pashley of Stratford-upon-Avon.
Royal Mail: Courier March 2005.

21

provided to lower the centre of gravity. Echoing the use of the horse-drawn 'Accelerators' in the 1830s used to speed Letter Carriers to outlying districts, a number of delivery staff can load their cycles and mail pouches into the back of vans to be transported to their 'walk'. From there, they can return to their office by cycle having completed their delivery.

Together with providing an efficient, cost effective mode of transport for the delivery of mail, the use of bicycles helps to lower Royal Mail's overall impact on the environment. Their practicality remains undiminished and so, over a hundred years after their adoption, they continue as a vital tool in delivering the mail.

Postmen with bicycles at the start of their rounds, circa 1920.
BPMA ref: E9347

Left:
Postwoman with a step-through bicycle, on a rural delivery route at Goodrich, near Hereford, 1949.
BPMA ref: P 4083

Right:
Postwomen with bicycles, Barnet, circa 1915
During World War I, women were recruited to replace postmen who joined the armed forces.
BPMA ref: P 6020

"I heartily dislike the notion of sending the boys out on red machines like imps from hell"
Post Office official discussing his dislike of red motor- bikes, favouring the standard BSA green 1932/3

Combinations and Tri-cars

In common with horse-powered services, the first motorcycles utilised by the Post Office were supplied under contract. Various models were used including a motor-tricycle made by the Eagle Engineering & Motor Co. Ltd. This petrol-driven machine first

Stamp booklet, 1993
Stamp book cover by Debbie Cook issued November 1993. Number one in a series of three. Motorised cycle-carrier depicted was the first motorised mail in Sittingbourne, Kent.
BPMA Philatelic collection

First motorised mail at Sittingbourne, circa 1902.
Motorcycle with trailer fitted with wicker basket. It served the villages Greenstreet, Doddington, Frinstead, Milstead and later Wormshill.
BPMA

saw service in London in 1903 and covered a daily distance of 35³/₄ miles at an average speed of 10 miles per hour. Its speed exceeded the lower speeds being attained by the petrol and electric vans being trialled at the time. Vans could however carry a far greater load. Further trials were held in 1906, with hired 'Motor Tricycle Carriers' on light mail services in London.

Early in 1914, a trial of an auto-wheel was carried out on a rural service in Watford. This was an ordinary bicycle with a small petrol-driven motor attached. Unfortunately, the vehicles suffered a considerable number of punctures, and following another trial in Douglas on the Isle of Man in 1920 which had similar results, further experiments with these were abandoned.

Later in 1914, following the successful use of motorcycles fitted with side carriers and driven by contractor's employees, the Post Office carried out their own experiments with similar machines. 20 vehicles were purchased and introduced on rural delivery and collection services with postman driving them. These comprised 10 New Hudson, 6 Douglas Brothers and 4 Rover Co. machines. They were found to be underpowered and unsuitable for the gradients experienced.

First rural post car used at Sittingbourne, Kent, 1910.
BPMA P5170

"considerable trouble is being experienced in working the service by motor-cycle"
A. Tydeman, 14 July 1915, POST 30/3358

Four 'Tri-Cars' were also purchased as replacements. Two each were supplied by the manufacturers Warrick & Co. and the Wall Auto-Carrier Co. and were assigned to work at Alnwick, Clitheroe, Chipping Norton and Chesterfield. This group of machines formed the genesis of the present day Royal Mail fleet.

A Post Office official discussing the previous experimentation with 'Tri-Cars', made the following observation in 1919:

Tri-car at Oakham Post Office, circa 1915. Used on Oakham to Pickwell motorised mail service. Manufactured by Warrick & Co., Reading. Together with the purchase of twenty combination motorcycles, these formed the genesis of the Royal Mail fleet. *BPMA P8030*

Rural motor-tricycle with front basket carrier at Clapham Post Office, circa 1905. *BPMA P8877*

"In regard to Tri-Cars, development has been at a standstill, of the two firms making tri-cars before the war, one, Auto Carriers, Ltd., have now designed a small 4 wheel car, and the other Messrs. Warricks, have hardly recovered from the disorganisation of their factory due to the war...It therefore seems necessary, until tri-cars are again put on the market in substantial numbers, to depend upon motor bicycles with side cars, or alternatively, upon four-wheeled vehicles...the immense production of cars of the Ford type has bought the first cost of the car, and the spares, to such a low figure that, for the heavier services, such cheap cars can compete with motorcycles...and I should be inclined to recommend a trial"
Post Office Stores Department, 6 March 1919

Solo machines

Following World War I, more reliable and higher-powered machines were available and use of such vehicles was extended to include town deliveries. In 1919, disquiet was being voiced in official quarters regarding the wisdom of allowing Postmen to drive the new vehicles:

> *"My own experience of Postmen as Drivers has not been satisfactory and the only really successful Motor Cycle posts have been those worked under Contract, for the Contractor either drives himself or provides a capable man...steps should be taken to employ only those who have aptitude and to give them a thorough training, Men selected who do not show aptitude should be sent back to Foot or Cycle posts"*
> Post Office Surveyor, 1919

The first experimental use of solo motorcycles commenced in 1924. These three $2^3/_4$ h.p. machines were adapted for postal use by the provision of a wire mesh rear pannier that was capable of containing a load of around 70lb of mail. By the following year around 400 motorcycles of various makes were in use on both delivery and collection work. These tended to take the place of the rural cycle posts. It was estimated that one postman with a motorcycle could cover the same ground as two postmen on pedal cycles.

Riders of solo machines in 1931, raised the issue of the dangerous nature of wet city roads. Authority was given to convert two of the four machines then in use in London; the remaining motorcycles were converted two years later in 1933. This was however only regarded as an experimental move. Although initially regarded as an economical option, motorcycles came to be compared unfavourably with the light motor vans. Motorcycle riders viewed their colleagues with envy as vans had a greater load capacity and provided better protection from the weather.

Post Office messengers on BSA motorcycles, 1933. *BPMA: H6808, Post Office Magazine, May 1934.*

In Leeds in 1933, boys of 17 years were allowed to volunteer to undergo training in the use of motorcycles for telegram delivery work, though parental approval was also necessary. 16 of the boys were selected and they quickly proved capable. There was some doubt at official levels whether riding motorcycles could prove to be hazardous to health:

"...riders should be further medically examined after they have performed the duties for six months in order that it may be ascertained whether motor cycling has any physical effects on growing youths" Post Office memorandum accompanying Circular No. 64/33, October 1933

Group of Telegraph Messengers on BSA motorcycles at Ealing, circa 1934. *BPMA P153*

Motorcycles were ideally suited to the telegram service, the fleet of which comprised almost exclusively of 125cc motorcycles. In February of the same year, a blizzard grounded almost all other transport services. The boys continued to get through on their mounts and the success of the scheme was assured. Additional services quickly commenced in other towns and cities. The vehicles came to be regarded with great affection by their riders, though tinged with an appreciation as to their foibles:

"last week she took me up Nob Hill on top just like a bloomin' nightingale, and I'd got a good load on 'er too. But she's never the same two days together boy. Now today she was a-snortin' like a blinkin' bacon pig, an' she wouldn't pull th' skin off a tapioca puddin'."
W.A. Hancock, The Post, 16 April 1932

Probably the most well known of all motorcycles used by the Post Office was the BSA Bantam. This small and popular motorcycle was first manufactured in 1948. Special GPO models were produced and engine sizes steadily increased from 125cc to 175cc. They were used for both telegraph and letters work, but production ceased in 1971. With the demise of this motorcycle, further trials were held with the smaller mopeds still available.

Mopeds
Raleigh Supermatic mopeds were introduced experimentally for use on postal work in 1962. Six mopeds were introduced initially, five taking the place of cycle deliveries in the Oxford area with a spare moped being held in reserve. This trial extended the following year to include Shrewsbury (one machine), Northallerton (three), Exmouth (one) and Newent (one) with additional spares in each area.

The experiment with mopeds was deemed a success and they were introduced as standard equipment in 1967. Initially, another 50 Raleigh's were ordered but these were regarded as very expensive; £148 each compared with £233 for a 50cf van. Honda mopeds were considered but there were additional reservations. One Post Office official referring to these machines went so far as to add:

"...we have not used a foreign vehicle on postal work before. Candidly, while I recognise the commercial argument, I find the idea of buying a Japanese machine rather unpatriotic..."
BPMA, POST 122/4473, 1967

The number of mopeds required was over estimated and rather than keep a large number in stock, the Motor Transport Division allocated a considerable number to Telegraph work instead. Raleigh then ceased manufacture of the Supermatic model, and the less elaborate Raleigh Runabout moped was purchased with an additional trial of Honda mopeds taking place.

A lack of suitable home-produced machines in more recent times has meant that brands such as Honda and Kawasaki have been utilised for Express services such as Datapost. Honda has also supplied 'quad bikes' to Royal Mail for use on more difficult terrains.

Expresspost service, 1981.
Honda 250cc motorcycle used for the priority Expresspost service, the rider, in radio contact with his office, delivered urgent papers etc. in the Hampstead area, 1981.
BPMA ref: 000518

Honda Quad-bike on
the Scottish island of
Kerrera in January
2002.
*Image: Royal Mail:
Courier*

Postman and BSA
solo motorcycle on
postal delivery work
near Tavistock 1929.
Fitted with a rear
carrier, these
machines enabled a
postman to carry out
the work of two cycle
posts and were a
cheaper alternative to
postal vans.
BPMA H6806

Motorcycle combination, 1932
This postman is making a collection with his BSA 499cc motorcycle. Difficulties could be experienced with the small capacity at times. Occasionally the postman found it was impossible to close the lid covering the mail stored in the sidecar.

Poster produced by
the Post Office to
advertise the Telegram
Service. Designed by
Pat Keely, 1950.
BPMA P109/32 IRP 22

"The Red Mail Van is the most ubiquitous of vehicles. It is found in the streets of the big towns, at the railway stations at dead of night, in the Devonshire lanes and on the wild roads of Stornoway ... Thirty years ago, practically the whole of the Post Office transport service was in the hands of contractors, and the Motor Van was hardly known; but the advent of the internal combustion engine has revolutionised all the conditions of this service. At the present time there is hardly a horse left and the Post Office services every year pass more and more from the hands of contractors to the direct control of the Post Office."
Director of Postal Services, January 1934

Early Choices: Steam, Electric and Oil

Towards the end of the 19th century, advances in technology meant that the Post Office was faced with an almost bewildering choice in possible modes of transport for the mails. The Post Office carried out several trials with a variety of vehicles, but continued to allow the contractor to bear the majority of the risk while advances were being made in the emerging forms of motorised road transport powered by steam, electricity and oil drives.

Each month seemed to have one manufacturer or another loudly proclaiming their latest product to be the most advanced of its type, although most such claims were destined to become a technological dead end. There was considerable prestige associated with a contract with the Post Office, and if a vehicle manufacturer was able to demonstrate to the buying public that a large and official body such as the Post Office favoured their vehicle over that of the opposition, sales would boom. As a consequence, many manufacturers were vying for official sanction of their machines. The Post Office was almost inundated with offers to carry the mails on various routes:

"Would you be prepared to consider a proposition for working your parcels post service by means of traction engines instead of horses? We are prepared to supply such engines to do the distance from London to Bedford for example, at the rate of 8 miles per hour, and at a cost less than half that of horses…"
J&H.McLaren, Manufacturer of Traction Engines, 2 January 1894

The Post Office also had to manage the incorporation of new vehicle technologies within the constraints of the law. The above suggestion was in breach of the Locomotive Act of 1865 which prohibited the running of traction engines on public roads at anything other than low speeds. Four miles per hour was permitted on the public highway, or two miles per hour through any city, town or village. Hardly the sorts of speeds that were going to attract the attentions of a service where speed was paramount.

Amendments to the Highways and Locomotives Act of 1878 further stipulated that one of the persons in charge of the locomotive was required to precede it by at least 20 yards to render assistance to horses and carriages. With such legal strictures in place, it is not surprising that advances in Post Office road transport also advanced at a similarly sedate pace.

The Post Office also considered suggestions for the use of electric vans to be used in the service of the mails:

"Our new Electric Parcel Van which has been running in the City very successfully for the past fortnight, is in our opinion specially adapted for the use of the Post Office…roughly half the cost of horse power…allow us to run our van…in the service of the Post Office in order to demonstrate its utility."
W.C.Bersey, E.J.Clubbe & Co. Electric Road Car Works, 13 March 1894

Unfortunately the 1878 Act also included electric vehicles. In view of this the Post Office advised E. J. Clubbe that they would await a change in the law before proceeding with any trials of their vans.

Returning to steam power, in 1896, the Post Office received the following proposal:

> "We have a motor vehicle...which we consider well arranged for Post Office work...we should be much pleased if you or any of your staff will favour us by inspecting the van"
> Julius Harvey & Co, 2 October 1896

The Post Office agreed to inspect Harvey & Co's steam-driven van and, after observing that the vehicle's capacity was little more than a third that of horse-drawn vans, the company offered to increase the van's size. It was tested on the service between London and Reigate from the 16 December 1897 for nine weeks, excluding an overhaul two-thirds of the way through the trial. The van assisted in the transport of Parcel Mails being carried by the over-burdened horse-drawn London and Brighton Parcel Coach. In his 1898 annual report the Postmaster General reported that, other than for a burst tube on one occasion, the van performed the journey well, being within the time permitted for a horse conveyance.

Also in 1896, Mr. Cockerell, a Post Office official, went to Reigate to observe the arrival of 20 motor vans taking part in the Motor-Car Club run from London to Brighton. He reported on his observations and made recommendations as to the vehicles' speed, ease of travel and suitability for Post Office work:

"... the first half dozen... came into the town at a high rate of speed, certainly more than 12 miles an hour. Nearly all of the cars were propelled by oil motors and gave off a very strong smell, but very little smoke. The principal objections to the cars, I considered to be the strong vibration to which most of them were subjected, the smell, and the buzzing noise of the machinery. The noise, though objectionable to the persons in the car, would otherwise serve the useful purpose of warning pedestrians and others of what would be otherwise a silent approach, the wheels being fitted with india-rubber tires... I noticed one light van, the Daimler Parcels van, which appeared suitable... for Post Office purposes"
P Cockerell, 16 November 1896

Daimler motor van, 1898. Used on the Reading-Newbury mailcart service.
BPMA C377

A steam tractor was obtained from Wallace & Steevens of Basingstoke in November 1904, for a four-week trial. Following a second successful trial, the Post Office Stores Department purchased the vehicle for £430. Running costs were estimated at £24 6s 8d per month compared with £37 per month horse hire. This was the first self-propelled vehicle owned by the Post Office, albeit for the Stores Department, and it entered continuous service late in 1905. It was sold nine years later for half of its purchase price.

In 1898, trials were also carried out with oil (petrol) driven cars. An oil motor car, the property of the British Motor Syndicate, was used for a week in October of that year for conveying mails between Post Office Headquarters and the South Western District Parcels Office, and again two weeks later for conveying parcel mails between the South Western District Office and Kingston-on-Thames. This service was said by the Post Office to have been carried with:

"great regularity and in somewhat less time than the horse conveyance ordinarily employed".

As the car was not specifically designed for the transport of mails the experiment was not continued. The British Motor Syndicate preferred to wait until they held a more suitable car before further trials were conducted.

Electrically-propelled motor cars had met with less success. A car owned by the Electrical Vehicle Syndicate was used on town work for four weeks where unfortunately two accidents led to severe delays. Despite this setback, other reports were favourable:

"So far as experiments went, they showed that motor cars were likely to prove in the near future a mode of conveyance for letter and parcel mails which would be attended with advantage both as regards speed and economy"
Report of the Postmaster General, 1898

Maudslay Stores 'No.1'
BPMA C299

A first purchase: 'Maudslay No. 1'

"I venture the opinion that no feature of postal or engineering work has undergone such a fundamental change and with such beneficial results to those services …as the method of dealing with the various activities of the Post Office. Motor transport is the agent which has made such changes possible."
Captain A. Hudson, Chief Motor Transport Officer to the Post Office, 1936

In March 1906, proposals were made to purchase a petrol-driven vehicle for carrying stores. This was Maudslay 'No. 1', a $2^{1}/_{2}$ ton van that entered service in January 1907 and proved enormously successful. In its 18 years' service, it covered some 300,000 miles and was eventually sold back to the Maudslay Motor Co. of Coventry for use in advertising.

Three more lorries were purchased in 1913/14 for use by the Stores Department. The Engineering Department purchased a car and a testing van for the use of Superintending Engineers and also took control of four second-hand cars.

Vehicles during World War I

During World War I a number of contractors who supplied vans used on postal business found themselves under increased pressure to meet the demands put upon them. In 1915, Treasury authority was given for governmental assistance towards meeting the increased cost of upkeep due to war conditions. Around 1916, the policy of subsidising contractors was modified. The prevailing attitude of 'business as usual' had begun to give way to the realisation that there was a need for strict economy of expenditure within the Post Office. Coupled with the introduction of compulsory military service, this led to a shortage of manpower. Such a labour-intensive service as the Post Office was hit hard.

A large number of long-distance road motor services had been introduced prior to the war, primarily for conveyance of parcels. The lighting restrictions on the roads imposed in January 1916, as a precaution against air raids, meant that the contractors were unable to run at the speeds necessary to meet the demands of their contracts. A great number of the services were therefore transferred to rail.

Vehicles were adapted to comply with the restrictions, their wings and bumpers were painted white to allow for greater visibility in the blackout and lights were masked. Telegraph messengers were required to make their way through the darkened streets with hooded headlights, their motorcycles also sporting white-edged mudguards as an aid to visibility.

The shortage of labour, petrol and fodder for horses also had an increased effect on the reliability of services and made it difficult to maintain accurate timetables. All of this meant that a steady diminution of services took place. Sunday despatches virtually ceased and road services in Scotland were reduced from six to three days a week.

Morris Z van, wartime adaptation to coal gas carried in an envelope above the vehicle. Also shows adaptions in response to blackout regulations.
BPMA neg 11624

By June 1916, petrol had become so hard to obtain that some Stores vehicles were adapted to run on coal-gas. They were described as:

"large clumsy affairs which flopped about on the tops of hoods and canopies. We were much amused at the sight of these gadgets when visiting London"
Major C. Wheeler, O.B.E., Chief Automobile Engineer G.P.O speaking in 1933

From July 1916, supplies of petrol were rationed. In common with other petrol consumers, motor mail contractors were required to apply for six-month licences. This worked effectively on the whole, although occasionally contractors had difficulties and were forced to borrow petrol until the required licences were produced. When actual shortages of petrol occurred, in some parts of the country it was obtainable from the local military authorities, and some contractors resorted to utilising buses, taxicabs or hire cars for the movement of mails. Whilst contractors experienced great difficulties in all of the large towns, it is all the more remarkable that such an efficient service continued in light of the large increase in the letter and parcel traffic resulting from the Expeditionary Forces. In order to meet this increase in demand, the London Postal Service had to rely on the aid given by the Army Postal Service and lorries lent by the War Office.

Where necessary, the Post Office assisted contractors by intervening to protect drivers and mechanics against enlistment when substitutes were unobtainable. Women were employed as drivers of horsed vehicles and there was increased remuneration for contractors to meet the increase in expenditure on wages, fodder for horses and petrol.

The War Office had been prompt in requesting an inspection of the horses owned by J. Allen, mail contractors to the Post Office, with a view to commandeering them for work with the Expeditionary Force. There followed an exchange of views between the Post Office and the War Office where it was pointed out that these animals were effectively carrying out the work of another government department. Any depletion in their numbers would cause a severe curtailment or delay in the postal services. Accepting the vital work in communication and morale provided by the Post Office, the War Office issued instructions not to commandeer any horses in Royal Mail services. A similar situation existed during World War II when the use of horse-drawn vans continued alongside the motor-driven fleet.

Following World War I, the Post Office purchased 40 motor lorries from the Ministry of Supplies to meet certain contingencies set up by as a result of the war. From April 1919, these lorries of which 35 were in daily use, were housed and run for a fixed charge by Tilling, one of the principal mail van contractors in London, on behalf of the Post Office. Tilling also provided 10 large vans for irregular work (including Foreign Mails). The vehicles, advanced for their time, would be regarded as quite primitive by today's standards. Many vehicles were fitted with solid tyres and drivers were exposed to the weather. A lack of adequate suspension combined with poor road surfaces often made a driver's life extremely uncomfortable.

The Post Office moves towards owning its own fleet

"It will no doubt be realised... that the Mail Van Service in London offers a most complicated problem when reorganising is contemplated and that it will take an appreciable period to prepare a satisfactory scheme when the work is taken in hand"
Report from Sir R. Bruce to the Post Office Secretary,
31 December 1919

Competition to win a contract from the Post Office to supply vehicles continued to be fierce between the contractors. By 1910, there were eight rival tenders for the SW, NW and Paddington Districts in London. Prior to World War I, the Post Office considered dispensing with contractors in London, Glasgow and other large towns in favour of a self-owned service. By the end of the war there were a large variety of vehicles in use on postal services. In 1919, the following types of van were being used:

Single Horse Van	10, 13 and 15cwt carrying capacity
Pair Horse Van	15, 20, 24 and 30cwt carrying capacity
Motor Van	12, 18, 20 and 25cwt carrying capacity

41

This variety had come about due to the differing instructions given to a number of contractors. The wide range of vans was thought to be inefficient and a reduction to three or four types was deemed necessary to create an efficient service. A report three years later recommended that there should be a reduction in (contractors) van types to just three:

Single Horse Van	20cwt
Pair Horse Van	30cwt
Motor Van	20cwt

In March 1919, the entire fleet of vehicles being used for mail services consisted of 20 motor-cycle combinations and four 'tri-cars'. The remainder of the Post Office fleet was not much larger; the Stores Department held 15 lorries (though they had the distinction of having owned the first), while the Engineering Department had seven cars and two testing vans. A combined total of 48 vehicles. Still, the Post Office relied in the main, on contractors. Totals for the principal London contractors are shown in the table below.

1920 Principal Contractors for the Conveyance of Mails in London

Contractor	Number of Motor Vans	Number of Horse Vans	Number of Horses
James Allen Ltd	-	257	500
Birch Brothers.	-	164	255
Mc Namara Ltd.	41	309	420
Thomas Tilling Ltd.	25	-	-
Leyland Motors	15	-	-

Consideration was given once more to a state-run service after the end of World War I. There was an official concern that the transport and Post Office unions might act in collusion to

squeeze greater concessions regarding working conditions from
the Post Office than was granted by the private contractors.

Some rural postmasters also expressed doubt about introducing
an unfamiliar technology:

> *"A good many Postmasters have, however, little or no knowledge of the
> workings of these machines having...the mistaken idea that motors
> are too complicated for the ordinary run of Postmen...when the fact
> that the handling of a modern motor vehicle can, after a little
> instruction, be mastered without much difficulty, by a Postman of
> ordinary intelligence...this misapprehension will be removed"*
> W Brown, Post Office Surveyor, 3 May 1919

Of primary consideration to the Post Office was the increase in
expenditure that a state-owned service would entail, not least in
wages. It was generally recognised that working conditions in the
Post Office were quite good, with reasonable hours and wages.
Contractors on the other hand were paid low wages and expected
long hours of work. Horse-van drivers' attendances were spread
over 72 hours each week. Horse-keepers also worked 72 hours
from Monday to Saturday and were expected to attend on
Sundays. Motor van drivers worked 63 hours per week before
overtime. The Post Office therefore proceeded with caution.

A new fleet owned and operated by the Post Office was intended
to replace all horse-drawn services. The large rise in the cost of
feed coupled with the smaller workforce and housing required for
motor services meant that an all-motorised fleet was the preferred
option. However, horse-drawn vans did remain in service until
after World War II and the last of the horse-drawn mail vans left
King Edward Building, London in 1949.

In 1920, 50 vans manufactured by GWK were purchased. These
small vans had a carrying capacity of some 8 cwt., and replaced
contract services in rural districts where an absence of

competition had led to what the Post Office regarded as
'*exorbitant charges*' by the contractors. They were initially
regarded a success, and authority was granted for the purchase of
another hundred with a load capacity of 10 cwt. the following
year. The decision turned out to be a mistake as their unique
friction drive power transmission proved to be a disappointment.
Mechanically, they were not up to the rigours of Post Office
work. Additionally, the lack of spare parts and service centres
proved incompatible with the demands of a Post Office fleet
steadily increasing in both size and miles covered. The Post
Office was forced to seek alternatives.

Ford and Morris Vehicles

The Post Office motorised fleet expanded rapidly during the
1920s. At this time it was only Ford and Morris vehicles that
were mass-produced with a countrywide repair service available.
It was therefore suggested that a fleet of Fords should be obtained
as a '*first purchase*', despite the fact that there had already been
vehicles purchased from a number of other manufacturers.

Some 200 1 ton Ford vans were duly purchased together with 14
Willys-Overland-Crossley vans of Canadian manufacture. These
were for work principally in urban areas. The mail contractors
were worried. They had been running a profitable contracted
service for a considerable time and it was now clear that the Post
Office was serious about running its own fleet.

Small, local trials continued. On 18 December 1923, Major
Wheeler of the Post Office Stores Department was granted
authority to purchase a single small Morris van in order that
"*a practical trial may be carried out on an ordinary Mail Service*".

By February 1925, the entire Post Office fleet comprised:

Postal:	553 Vans
	228 Motorcycles
Engineering:	257 Vans
	731 Motorcycles
Stores:	50 Vans

The fleet totalled 1819 vehicles, 663 of these were manufactured by the Ford Motor Company Ltd in England. Differences, such as near-side steering and controls in a foreign make like Ford, were acceptable to the Post Office in view of their very low purchase cost, and the moderate running and maintenance costs the vans were considered to have. More importantly to the public, it was officially expressed by the Post Office that:

"...they do their work well..."
Report to the GPO by Mr P. H Patterson (L.&N.W Rly), 1922

However, purchasing from what was deemed in essence an American company, was regarded as extremely unpatriotic in some quarters. The Postmaster General frequently had to answer questions on the subject in Parliament:

"if he can state...whether motor-vehicles of Foreign manufacture are at present being ordered by the postal service; and, if so, will he take steps to ensure that only motor-vehicles which have been produced entirely by British labour and capital will be employed in the future?"
MP to PMG, 11 February 1925

In response Post Office officials insisted in July 1925 that:

"...no wholly British van known to us at present can take the place of the Ford for mail services..."
BPMA, File Reg. No. 230,806/25

45

Left:
Artwork for 1985
stamp issue
Unadopted artwork
submitted for the
1985 stamp issue
celebrating '350
years of Royal Mail
Public Postal Service'.
Design highlights the
link between road
and rail transport,
1985.
BPMA ref: FC169/005

Right:
Morris Minor on
front cover of leaflet
'News-information',
looking at Motor
Transport in the Post
Office, October 1963.
BPMA Portfolio
collection

Despite this, the Post Office came under pressure to seek a British-made alternative to the Ford vehicles. Experiments in 1925 with 10 of the comparatively new British-made Morris vans at Peterborough failed, the vans spending a great proportion of the first five months out of commission. Within two years events took a turn. Ford ceased manufacture of their T and TT Models and, by 1927 nearly all motor mail vans purchased were made by Morris. The Post Office did purchase the 130 cu ft Ford Van, 56 of which were in service in 1930. However, the cramped conditions caused by their low roofs and small bodies proved unpopular with postmen.

Morris rapidly gained favour with the Post Office and their vehicles began to dominate the fleet, particularly their famous 'Bullnose' van. The company's products quickly proved their worth and Morris remained a large supplier of vehicles to the Post Office for a considerable number of years. A large number of former Post Office workers alive today fondly recall that most ubiquitous of post World War II vans, the Morris Minor.

Vehicles during World War II

During World War II some Post Office vehicles were employed
for alternative uses in times of emergency. The two Mobile Post
Offices introduced just prior to World War II were used briefly as
mobile recruiting stations, credited with securing almost 1500
volunteers for the civil defence in their six-week campaign.
Following this, they were used as 'mobile coast stations'. Kept as
reserves at Cambridge and Harrogate, these contained
transmitting and receiving equipment to maintain contact with
ships and were ideally suited to travel to cover any permanent
station around the coast put out of action by enemy action.

Enemy fire would
occasionally render a post
office unusable, and special
tented post offices were
developed that could offer a
range of counter services
when required. Each portable
office travelled in adapted
Royal Mail vans.

Morris Z Type in
wartime livery to
comply with blackout
regulations during
World War II.
BPMA

Factories found it difficult to
maintain the supply of
special coach built bodies on
the smaller vans they were
providing, and so the Post

Scammell 'Mechanical
Horse', Aberdeen,
1942-3.
Used for the transport
of mail between office
and railway stations.
BPMA ref: neg 12538

Office was forced to accept the standard factory-built bodies
instead. Even following the war, this became standard as regards
the smaller vans being purchased. The majority of the vehicles
also became somewhat dilapidated following a lack of
maintenance. It took some years after the war to bring the fleet
up to its previous pristine appearance.

Royal Mail Morris 'Z type' vans outside Yeading repair and paint shop. During World War II, vehicles became badly run-down due to a lack of maintenance, circa 1950.
BPMA ref: P4685

Getting the Right Size and the Right Engines

Lessons learnt by the Post Office in the early days of owning its own fleet were followed in later years. Smaller types of postal and engineering vehicles had standard manufacturers' bodies modified to suit the specific requirements of the jobs they were used for. While for the larger vehicles, special bodies were coach-built to a Post Office design and fitted to a standard chassis. Having a fleet of similar van body-types was regarded as being the most efficient practice to follow, as it allowed inter-changeability of vehicles between various classes of work, as the following statement by the Post Office from 1929 illustrates:

> *"The importance of homogeneity and interchangeability of type is*
> *such that changes regarded as necessary to meet conditions peculiar*
> *to London and perhaps a few other towns in the provinces have been*
> *adopted generally for all vans..."*
> BPMA, POST 33/3358A. 1929

Heavier vehicles were purchased from Albion (popular with the Telephones side of operations), and also from Commer, Austin, Maudslay, Morris and Seddon. While Morris had proved to be a favoured manufacturer, the Post Office was always reluctant to favour complete standardisation as it made them dependent on a single manufacturer. This could prevent competitive pricing and any shortages or industrial action would be immediately felt, with potentially grave repercussions to the postal service.

Standardisation also prevented any comparison of makes and
made them vulnerable to accusations of preferential treatment.

*"In view of all the evidence, we should like to accept the diesel engine
standard for all new heavy postal vehicles"*
Memo from E. G. Hucker to C. E. Calceley, Chief Motor Transport
Officer, Engineering Department (M Branch), June 1958

In 1955, trials began with diesel-engine vehicles for postal
purposes. A favourable report on these trials, submitted two years
later, approved further usage and authority was given for 50
diesel-engine vans to be purchased and operated side by side with
petrol-engine vehicles. The vehicles consisted of 25 240 cu. ft.
and the same number of 360 cu. ft. vans, all supplied by Morris.
In 1958, the trials concluded that large savings in fuel costs could
be realised by switching to diesel motors. Disadvantages such as a
slightly higher initial vehicle cost and vibration while ticking over
were thought not important enough to stand in the way of a
general switch of engine type. Diesel-engine vans quickly
replaced petrol, but it was not until the 1980s that an all-diesel
fleet policy was adopted.

At the start of the 1960s, a number of experimental road services
commenced. Conveying parcels in 600 cu. ft. vehicles, these
short-lived pilot studies took place in North Kent, the West
Riding area and the Thames Valley. It was found that transferring
the mails from the railways to road could provide a more efficient
service and over five million parcels were diverted from the
railways. From these experiments lessons were learnt. Problems
arose with large lorries attempting to gain access to sorting office
yards and loading platforms that decades earlier had only been
expected to handle horsed vehicles.

In contrast, some routes favoured still larger vehicles in order to
accommodate the increase in the number of parcels now being
carried by roads. Some permanent special road operations

resulted. In 1963, the new East Anglian Road Scheme had seen the purchase of 20 ton Morris motive units and large trailers, each with a load capacity of 1,300 cu. ft. These vehicles carried parcel mails (mostly at night) to and from seven parcel mail concentration centres: London, Peterborough, Norwich, Ipswich, Chelmsford, Cambridge and Southend-on-Sea.

The loose loading of mailbags was replaced with bulk containerisation and wheeled containers supplemented cages on pallets. The earlier wooden 'MATES' (Mail All-Purpose Trolley Equipment) were replaced with the special metal 'York' cages originally designed for transport of mails on the railways, which took their name from the city where they were developed.

Not all experiments or trials proved successful or popular. First discussed prior to World War II and again in 1954, a limited trial was eventually held with a Road TPO (Travelling Post Office) Scheme in 1961. Mirroring a similar practice on the railways, the TPO would have run on a Reading-Bristol route. It was to utilise a 1,700 cu ft. articulated vehicle travelling at 30 miles per hour with two postal staff in the rear sorting letters into pigeon holes. A subsequent lack of enthusiasm by some Post Office officials resulted in the abandonment of the scheme after only one trial run had taken place.

Centre page spread from the publication 'A look at Royal Mail's vehicle fleet' produced in 1993, illustrates the simple range of vehicles adopted by Royal Mail by the 1990s.
BPMA Portfolio collection

The earlier range of smaller vehicle weight classes has changed in more recent years with standard sizes of letter carrying vehicles now at 100, 225, 400 and 740 cu ft. With the demise of the post war Morris Minor, the last being delivered in 1972, Royal Mail struggled to find an alternative small capacity van. In 1970, the mail van fleet consisted of 11,500 50 cu ft vehicles, 2,000 of which were replaced each year. An experiment in economies was held at this time when 50 Mk III Reliant Super 5 cwt. three-wheeled vehicles were purchased for delivery work. This followed 3,000 miles of road trials but ultimately the experiment was an abject failure despite savings in Road Tax. This was primarily due to their instability and an accident when one vehicle burnt out. They were all disposed of after only three years service and a return to four-wheeled vehicles was made.

Reliant three-wheeled van.
BPMA

Livery has long been important to the Post Office fleet, clearly signifying the day-to-day activities of the organisation to the public at large. When the Post Office was responsible for the telephones in the early 20th century, the red colour of the postal delivery vehicles distinguished them from the green-liveried utility vehicles. National identity is now celebrated in Wales with a bi-lingual livery, and in Scotland with vehicles that carry the Scottish Crown. Other liveries have attempted to raise the public's awareness of new services and even Royal Mail's 'green' credentials.

Size of the Fleet

Today, Royal Mail is the owner of one of the largest road transport fleets in Europe. The costs of purchasing, maintaining and running its vehicles are now the driving force behind decision-making. In recent years it has been enough to adopt standard vans and lorries as produced by manufacturers with minimal alteration. In 1997, Royal Mail introduced a new vehicles management division named Vehicle Services, which is responsible for maintaining the fleet of some 30,000 vehicles.

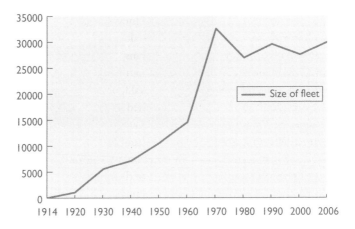

The size of the postal fleet has increased considerably since its inception. Following the lead of the Post Office Stores Department in 1906 in purchasing their own vehicles, a mails fleet began in 1914. Comprising just fourteen vehicles in that year, Royal Mail continued to rely in the main on contractors. The balance began to shift following World War I when large numbers of vans became available, coupled with increased power and reliability. By the beginning of World War II, the postal fleet had risen to 7,685 vehicles. A high of 33,100 was reached in 1972. By 2006 this had reduced slightly to 30,164

Cutting down on pollution

The annual distances covered by the Royal Mail fleet are vast. As long ago as 1927, they stood at approximately 10 million miles, 1 million of which were in the London postal area alone. By 1982, the number of miles being covered by the national postal fleet had risen to 320 million.

In 1990, a range of green 'Concept' vehicles was introduced. These provided the test bed on which a number of environmentally friendly features could be tried. In 1999, it was announced that Royal Mail had entered into partnership with the Ford Motor Company and BP to undertake a trial of low-emission vans. This involved 21 Ford Transit mail vans being converted to run on either compressed natural gas or liquefied petroleum gas. This followed another trial four years earlier when five Royal Mail Escort vans were converted to run on rapeseed methyl-ester. 30,000 miles were covered and provided essential information as to its suitability in an operational role. The trial was carried out at a time when the duty on this fuel was zero. Despite favourable results, the full rate of diesel duty was subsequently imposed and it became an uneconomic commercial proposition.

The impact that a road fleet can have on the environment can be extremely damaging. The Royal Mail vehicle fleet at the beginning of this century were producing 425,707 tonnes of CO_2 per annum. A restructured network with less road miles was introduced in an attempt to reduce this, and a 19% reduction was achieved within six years.

Such savings may prove difficult to sustain. In June 2003, the announcement was made by Royal Mail that it was to introduce a more efficient, linked transportation network. This was to include road, air and rail. However, when agreement could not be reached with English, Welsh and Scottish Railway (EWS), the rail element of the transportation of mail was removed. Efficiency on the rails had been steadily declining. On some routes, particularly to Scotland, more than 10 trains in every 40 carrying mail arrived late. Traditionally large quantities of mail had been simply transported by rail. The great majority of these were transferred to the roads and air. On other trains (Travelling Post Offices) postal staff carried out sorting of mail while the trains were in motion. This also ceased. The last sorting of mail on the railways took place on the 9 January 2004. While the move from rail to road may have been the cheapest and most efficient option, it remains to be seen what environmental impact such a change will have.

Despite the development of more efficient conventional engines, fuel costs for Royal Mail have continued to increase over the years. From almost 61$^1/_2$ million litres used in 1972, this had risen to over 100 million litres by 2006. Experimentation by Royal Mail with alternative fuel sources continues. A major trial involving 10% of Royal Mail Network operations vehicles commenced in 2005, this utilised bio-diesel, a 95% diesel/5% bio blend. Bi-fuel vehicles have now been purchased together with Honda IMA Hybrid vehicles and, in 2006, 147 LPG (Liquefied Petroleum Gas) vehicles operated in London and Perth.

Refuelling with Liquified Petroleum Gas (LPG) at Mount Pleasant, London, 2005. Following a successful trial, these vans entered regular service.
BPMA

Clockwise from top:

i) First Post Office vehicle fleet prior to World War I
Studd Street Stores Department in London: Wallis and Stevens Traction Engine (Stores 5), Ryknield van (Stores 4), Halley van (Stores 3), Alldays and Onions (Stores 2) and the very first new vehicle purchased by the Post Office in 1906, Maudslay lorry (Stores 1). Standing on the left is Major Wheeler, aptly named; he was instrumental in championing the purchase of vehicles by the Post Office.
BPMA ref: 53272

ii) Motor Transport Workshop, Studd Street, London. BPMA

iii: Morris Commercial. 105 cubic feet capacity, these vehicles were used in large numbers by the Post Office prior to World War II, 1934.
BPMA 9011

iv: Iveco Ford. Motor Transport Service Bulletin specifying vehicle livery, December 1987.
BPMA Portfolio collection

Left: Mail vans gathered in the yard at King Edward Building, London. Most of these would have been run by the mail contractors such as Mc Namara, 1931.
BPMA Neg. 7457

Right: Parcelforce Worldwide van.
Image: Royal Mail Vehicle Services, 2006

UNAUTHORISED USE OF OFFICIAL MOTOR VEHICLES

1. You must never use an official vehicle for an unauthorised purpose. For example: you must not take one away for private reasons, or depart for a private purpose from an official route, or carry without authority goods or passengers, whether or not they are Post Office employees. On journeys with no specified route, take the shortest practicable: if in doubt, consult your supervising officer.

2. Unauthorised use of official motor vehicles is regarded most seriously and you would not only expose yourself to severe disciplinary action—including dismissal—but also to prosecution, for instance, for using a vehicle that is not insured or for taking it away without the consent of the owner. The penalty on conviction might be very severe; perhaps a heavy fine or imprisonment, as well as suspension of your driving licence. If you were to have an accident in such circumstances you might be liable for its consequences also, and they could be very grave indeed.

3. If, by force of circumstances, you have to use an official vehicle in a way which might constitute a breach of these instructions, say in giving assistance after an accident, give a complete report to your supervising officer at the first opportunity afterwards.

P 570 E
(Revd 34994/54)
Wt. 73006   Gp. 844

Post Office notice warning employees against the unauthorised use of official motor vehicles. 1954.
BPMA ref. POST 68

The sheer variety of vehicles that has been utilised by the Post Office is quite staggering. Appendix 1 lists the different vehicles assigned to various Post Office departments in 1959. In addition to the expected vans and lorries used for moving the mail it includes others such as: forklifts, cranes, trench excavators, tippers, tractors, a radio station, mobile telegraph and post offices, ambulances and breakdown trucks and even amphibious vehicles. Where a manufacturer could not supply a ready-built design, Post Office architects and engineers would produce a design that met the organisation's diverse requirements.

Postal operations can range from intensive city centre collection and deliveries, to a rural postman delivering a single letter to a lone cottage on the moors. The mails are transported from one end of the country to the other as well as overseas. As a result of such diversity in its operations, Royal Mail has had the opportunity to experiment with the provision of more cost-effective methods of road transport on a very localised basis. Sometimes trials have proved unsuccessful such as the short-lived experiment in providing Travelling Post Offices on the road, where it was envisaged that Postmen would sort mail in the back of an articulated road vehicle. Other experiments have proved more successful, including the introduction of Postbuses that provide a highly regarded lifeline to isolated communities. Four such specialised developments are covered in greater depth here.

The first two have become a vital link with the community, each providing a different service. The third example was simply a short-lived advertisement of a new service, and the fourth possibly points toward the future of the entire Royal Mail fleet.

Postbus

Poster advertising the 'First Royal Mail Post Bus in Kent' that ran between Canterbury and Crundale.
BPMA Philatelic collection

Ride the Royal Mail Post Bus

E℞R   Royal Mail Post Bus

Canterbury to Crundale Service

from **Canterbury Bus Station** *calling at*
Thruxted, Godmersham, Crundale and Solestreet

mornings   MONDAY to SATURDAY
afternoons   MONDAY to FRIDAY

Times tables available at local Post Offices and the Bus Station

The First Royal Mail Post Bus in Kent

"Postbuses collect you and your mail"
Royal Mail website, 2006

The roots of the modern Postbus service lie in the mail coaches that used to convey both passengers and mail across the country. They provided the model and inspiration for the introduction of a similar service on a motorised basis in more modern times. While the last mail coach from London ran in 1846, it was not until 1967 that the first Postbus service was introduced in Wales.

Postbuses combine the delivery and collection of mail with regular stops to take on and drop off passengers. By this means Royal Mail is able to provide a vital service to some of the more isolated communities in the country. There were some similar services prior to 1967, but these tended to be actual bus services where the bus company had been contracted to carry mail for the Post Office in locked containers. Such services were often carried out in remote areas of Scotland.

Following the Report of the Committee on Rural Bus Services (Jack Report) published by the Ministry of Transport, the Post Office agreed with the Ministry in 1966, to run six postal minibuses experimentally. Replacing the normal mail van and travelling over the same route and to the same timings, each minibus was adapted to carry seven fare-paying customers.

Postbus Ticket issued 17 September 1974, *BPMA Philatelic collection*

The first Royal Mail Postbus service commenced on 20 February 1967, based at Llanidloes in Mid-Wales. The vehicle used was a Morris J2M16 minibus. This type of bus had been used extensively by the Post Office, with some 75 having been used as 'crewbuses'. The Llanidloes service was followed by the addition of further services in Devon (Honiton – Dunkeswell – Luppitt) introduced October 1967, the Lake District (Penrith – Martindale) introduced in October 1967 and East Lothian (Dunbar – Innerwick) introduced in June 1968.

Inauguration of the Post Bus service, Llanidloes, Wales, 20 February 1967. Shows the driver, Mr. J.S.Owen and his first passengers. Vehicle was a 7-seater Morris J2, registration KVB 103D, modified for the Post Office at the Cosely workshops. *BPMA Philatelic collection, MPH 9*

The service very nearly ground to a halt in its early stages. A Post
Office Steering Group paper on 'The Post Office and Rural
Transport' produced in 1970 made a number of observations
relating to the Postbus service. These included the observation that:

*"to extend the use of them further for purely social reasons would
delay the mail, create difficulties with Post Office Unions, lower security
standards and possibly increase costs"*
BPMA, POST 10/313

Despite this, not only did these trial services stay, but additional
routes were added. Reflecting the rural locations of some services,
Land Rovers were purchased in 1969/70. These could not seat
more than four people but were more suited to rougher terrain,
particularly in Scotland. Services are tied to national standards
for delivery and collection of mail, which has to take priority over
the service provided for passengers.

Over the years, a number of different vehicles have been utilised

Land Rovers
Royal Mail has
operated a number of
4x4 Landrovers to
support mail delivery
more remote delivery
locations. In 2006 over
100 of these were in
use by Royal Mail
including a number
that doubled as Post
Buses, as seen in this
line up.
*Image: Royal Mail
Vehicle Services 2006*

for this service. These have included Bedford CF, Commer
2000LB, Marina and Avenger estate cars and those workhorses of
the fleet: the Sherpa/Leyland Daf (later LDV). The service has
not only persevered but flourished in some areas. It continues to
provide a vital link for isolated communities that have lost any
other form of public transport. Frequently, a driver will look for
the signs that he will be returning with a passenger:

Postbus and driver, Tim Kimber at Wormshill near Sittingbourne, Kent, 2006
BPMA E920-1

"I know my regulars…they leave trolleys out or an open door, if I'm running late they ring each other up and ask have you seen him yet?"
Tim Kimber, Postbus Driver, Sittingbourne-Wormshill (route 300), 2006

In 2005, there were 166 Postbus routes around the country carrying 148,390 passengers over 3.3 million miles on 72,000 journeys. Illustrated guides are available detailing current routes and times. Services are tied to national standards for delivery and collection of mail which has to take priority over the service provided for passengers.

Vauxhall Brava Postbus (4x4)
One of the first such vehicles to enter service. The Brava is Royal Mail's main off road vehicle and a replacement for the ageing Land Rovers. It is used to deliver mail over difficult terrain such as experienced in the Scottish Highlands. This particular vehicle is used on the postbus service.
Image: Royal Mail, Vehicle Services

The Mobile Post Office

Cover of advertising booklet for new Mobile Post Office service published 1937

"I am very glad that the 'Post Office on Wheels' was able to make its debut at Marden and I hope that we shall be able to make a real contribution to the success of this and similar events by this latest example of our policy of getting into touch with the public"
Major G.C. Tryon, Postmaster General, 8 October 1936

During the 1930s, the Post Office Headquarters Department decided that there was a need for the provision of telegraph, telephone and postal facilities at special events such as race meetings and shows held at various locations around the country. It was felt that an 'office on wheels' would best meet this need.

Registered envelope serviced at the Mobile Post Office that attended the Daily Mail Golf Tournament April 7-10 1937. This envelope was posted on the first day of the event and the stamps have been cancelled with one of the special handstamps supplied to the mobile offices.
BPMA Philatelic collection

A need for manoeuvrability, safety, space and economy dictated an articulated vehicle. The towing unit selected for this purpose was a Morris Commercial Leader 3-ton tractor unit. It was given the registration index GPO 1, these particular letters being allocated to the Post Office for use on 'special' vehicles.

The lines of the tractor were designed to flow into that of the trailer. Painted in red and black, the mouldings and monogram were picked out in gold. Much attention was paid to the fittings of the trailer. There were three windows for transactions at the three postal and telegraph counters on the nearside of the vehicle which was equipped with two telephone cabinets, a generator, a teleprinter, a counter, stamp machines, a letter chute and mail bags.

Following its inauguration on 30 September 1936, GPO 1 made its first appearance at the Marden and District Commercial Fruit Show held at Marden, Tonbridge on 6-8 October that year. It was an immediate success and the introduction of a second Mobile Post Office (GPO2) was approved the following year.

> "...fully justified on prestige and other grounds"
> Post Office Board, 20 July 1937

Mobile Post Offices were used extensively in their earlier years. In its first nine months of service, between 6 October 1936 and 6 July 1937, GPO 1 appeared on 59 days at 23 events.

Mobile Post Office 'GPO 2' alongside the cruise-liner Queen Elizabeth. *BPMA*

During World War II Mobile Post Offices were transferred to war service, first used by the Home Office as mobile recruiting stations for the Civil Defence, then by the Engineering Department of the Radio Branch as reserve mobile radio receiving and transmitting stations. After the war, a third Mobile Post Office was introduced with a Morris FF unit utilising the GPO registration. However despite Seddon motive units replacing the earlier Morris towing vehicles in 1957, the earlier vehicles were becoming worn out. Three caravan-type trailers, each towed by a Karrier Gamecock tender, were introduced in the early 1970s. The introduction of permanent telephone kiosks at racecourse and other locations coincided with a declining need for their presence and the three offices only appeared at sixteen events in 1985.

Design brief for 'mega-unit' Mobile Post Office introduced in the 1980s.
BPMA Portfolio

A new type of mobile post office entered service in 1984. This was a 'mega-unit' that could function both as a post office, complete with a service counter, but also as an exhibition area with separate hospitality suite.

There has been a recent resurgence in mobile post offices since 1996. A smaller type of van entered service. Instead of visiting events and shows, these green-liveried vehicles visit a number of towns on a regular basis bringing Post Office Counters services to the public where they no longer have access to a post office.

Left:
Mobile Post Office
The beginning of the
21st century saw the
introduction of a new
type of Mobile Post
Office. These smaller
vans were more
suited to serving a
number of villages
and towns on a
timetabled circuit.
*Image: Royal Mail
Vehicle Services 2006*
Right:
New Mobile Post
Offices awaiting
transfer to their
regions. Note Welsh
livery applied to the
centre vehicle.
*Image: Royal Mail
Vehicle Services 2006*

Royal Air Mail Service

*"There is a sufficiency of air mail work in London (including runs to
and from Croydon Aerodrome) to justify the provision and use of these
vans for this purpose alone"*
BPMA, POST 33/4709, Internal memo. 1934

A special fleet of Royal Mail vans was introduced in June 1930 to
handle and advertise the new Royal Air Mail service. 137 special
pillar boxes were provided in various locations around the UK.
These boxes and the new vans were painted blue.

Eight Morris Minor vans were introduced for collection duties,
and two 105cu ft vans for the conveyance of mails. One of these
was supposed to be replaced with a 250cu ft van in 1935, but the
larger van was simply added to the fleet instead.

Morris Air Mail Van,
one of the short-lived
blue vans introduced
for the collection and
transport of air mail,
1930-38.
BPMA

65

The streamlined air mail car delivering mail to a waiting aircraft (De Haviland DH84) at Liverpool aerodrome, 1935. *BPMA ref: POST 118/28*

An additional van took the form of a special promotional car, its streamlined body designed by sculptor Maurice Lambert. Lambert was suggested by Mr. Beddington, a Post Office official, because he had designed an aeroplane figure *"for some exploit of Sir Malcolm Campell's"*. The special bodywork, constructed by the Duple Coachworks, was mounted on a standard 15cwt Morris chassis.

"Special fast collection services by Air Mail motor vans are arranged to connect with the main Air Mail despatches from London during the day"
The Kentish Mercury, 4 October 1935

In 1932, it was also suggested that the newly introduced BSA motorcycles, purchased for the day delivery of telegrams should be painted with the new '...*air mail blue which is quite an attractive and distinctive colour.*' It was not then known however if the air mail scheme was to be a success, so the standard BSA green was adopted instead.

One of the special Morris air mail vans, a 10cwt, 70 cubic feet capacity vehicle, leaving the Customs House, Croydon Airport, 1933. *BPMA ref: P8560*

Due to the increased use of the service, and an expansion of the '*blue box system*' in 1934, a complete revision of the existing blue van collection services was made. An increase in the number of vans being required, the fleet was expanded to 26 Morris Minor vans in 1935, with the three larger vans continuing to support the service and the promotional van being used just for publicity purposes. There were also three reserve vans. Some services were occasionally substituted by red vans on a strictly temporary basis.

Air Mail leaflet. Explanatory leaflet issued by Post Office regarding use of Air Mail Boxes, 1930-38. *BPMA Philtelic collection PH10*

The winter of 1935 saw four of the vans unused due to a decreased workload. The following February, the three reserve vans were withdrawn from the service and repainted red to join other duties. A reserve force was provided in June when another four were withdrawn from regular service.

Transfer of mail from the Royal Mail airmail delivery van into the awaiting aeroplane, Croydon, 1930-38. *BPMA*

"If the blue pillar boxes are to be abolished, it would seem that the streamline blue car would no longer be required"
Engineering Department, M.T.B., August, 1938

In August 1938, instructions were issued for all Minor vans to be withdrawn from airmail service. They were repainted red and entered normal service by the end of the year. At the end of 1938, the streamlined van was put on display at the Glasgow Empire exhibition. After this it was returned to London, having covered 30,000 miles on its duties. It was no longer required for its original purpose. The special body was removed and replaced with a standard 105 cu. ft. body more suited to normal postal duties. Although short-lived, the special blue vans had provided an interesting and worthwhile diversity to the regular postal fleet.

Electricars' tow-truck, Ideal for indoor work. Seen here towing a line of 'hay-carts' loose filled with mail bags.
BPMA 000083

Electric Vehicles

"...it is better to commence these experimental services with light loads and short distances and gradually to increase the distance covered as the capabilities of the Motor Car are proved."
London Postal Section, 5 September 1902 referring to the use of electrically-powered mail vans

Royal Mail currently operates over 30,000 vehicles in their commercial fleet and an additional 2,600 company cars. As a result there is a very real need to reduce the impact that such an enormous fleet has on the environment, and the use of electrically-powered vans is one way in which emissions can be reduced. There has been extensive use of electrically-powered vans in recent years, but prior to this, the greatest period of experimentation was both before and immediately following World War II.

Daimler electric mail van, 1899.
BPMA ref. P11075

The Post Office had been experimenting with electric vehicles for over a hundred years. When the adoption of motorised vehicles into the service was first suggested, it was electrically-powered vans that were initially thought the most suitable. In 1901, Julius Harvey and Co. had supplied an Electric Oppermann Mail Van to the Post Office and this was used quite successfully for inter-district and station services in London for over a month in 1901 and for 10 days during July of the following year. It ran at some 12 miles per hour and covered over 30 miles per day. Despite successful trials, the Post Office refused to commit themselves at this time. Following favourable reports from the British however, the French Post Office purchased their own fleet of electric vans in 1903.

The reduction of emissions was not initially the primary aim of these earlier trials, which instead highlighted two effective operational uses for electric trucks and tractors. One was the transporting of the mails to and from railway stations. Since 1913/14 about 35 trolleys powered by electric batteries had been introduced at important mail centres when post offices were frequently situated adjacent to the stations. Staff were thereby relieved of much of the heavy manual labour associated with delivery and receipt of the large volumes of mail transported by rail at that time.

Authority was given in August 1920 for the purchase of 13 electric battery trucks to be supplied by The English Electric Co. Ltd for conveying letter and parcel mails between

One of three electromobile battery powered postal vans used at Leeds, 1928.
BPMA ref. H6811

Stamp booklet, 1994
One of three stamp book covers by Debbie Cook issued September 1994. Number three in 'Postal Vehicles' series of three depicts an experimental electrically powered van.
BPMA Philatelic collection

Experimental electric mail van, probably Leeds, 1932. Third in a series of postal vehicles illustrated by Debbie Cook Printed by Harrison & Sons Limited

£2
Royal Mail Stamps
Eight at 25p

the Birmingham Sorting Office and the New Street Railway
Station. Delivery of the vehicles began in September 1922 and
was completed in March 1923. Another truck was delivered to
the sorting office in 1935 following a successful trial of a 10cwt
Greenbat Electric truck the previous year. This was a 1-ton
capacity Greenbat Fixed Platform Electric Battery Truck from
Messrs. Greenwood and Batley. Trials of three of the 'new type'
electric trucks also commenced at Leeds for conveyance of mails
between the sorting office and the railway stations.

Early trials with larger vans had determined that their initial high
cost proved unfavourable in comparison with that for a petrol
vehicle. Additionally, their mileage range was limited and the
need to recharge batteries meant that the vehicles were often out
of service for the greater part of the day. Any time that a mail
vehicle spent off the road could have expensive repercussions. In
1926, four 25cwt petrol Bean mail vans, being operated under
contract by James Allen Ltd, were averaging $22^1/_2$ hours each on
the road per day, this in the thick of London traffic. Any electric
vehicle available at the time would simply not have been capable
of delivering the required workload. It can be seen that any
adoption of electric vehicles had to be carefully planned.

Pedestrian controlled
Electric Delivery
Truck, Battersea,
1954. These delivery
trucks, primarily for
parcels, but also used
for letter mails.
BPMA P19347

In 1928, a small fleet of seven Victor electric vans entered service
at Mount Pleasant in London, for the conveyance of mails. These
were in use for around five years before being replaced with more
conventional engine vans as their running costs proved unfavourable.

Another successful use of electrically-powered vehicles was the
Pedestrian-controlled Electric Delivery Truck (PEDT).
Introduced in 1954, the vehicles were fitted with a box body and
lockable sliding doors. They were used for parcel delivery work at
first, and later on town letter deliveries. These reduced the strain
on the delivery staff while offering a large secure storage area far
in excess of that possible for a postman with a wheeled trolley.
In 1978, the Post Office had 470 electric trucks on postal duties.
At the beginning of the 21ˢᵗ century, the use of a smaller variant
was extended across the country.

The slow speed of electric vehicles, particularly on hills, has
traditionally been found to be detrimental to mail delivery
operations. More recently, developments in design and efficiency
mean that this is no longer the case. In 1995, Royal Mail carried
out a 30-month trial with Ford's Ecostar battery-driven vehicles,
which ran on sodium sulphur batteries that could be charged in
seven hours and provided a range of 100 miles. In a news release
it was announced:

*"Before long electric vehicles are going to be part of our lives. It is vital
for an organisation like Royal Mail to help develop them for general
use and we are delighted to be joining in Ford's test programme"*
Mike Horlor, Head of Royal Mail Transport, 1995

The trial took place in London and Oxford, the latter being the
test bed for another experiment with an electric vehicle the
Bradshaw Carryall. Proving useful for deliveries in the city centre
in 2006, three of these vans remain in regular use and are both
practical and popular with their drivers. The installation of on-
site wind generators for recharging the vehicles is being

71

investigated to further decrease the impact on the environment. As local authorities introduce ever more stringent restrictions on vehicle usage or introduce congestion charges such as in Central London, operational lessons learnt with alternative fuel vehicles will prove invaluable.

"The electric vehicle provides the best chance of meeting the future vehicle emission and noise demands in the most sensitive urban areas"
Postal Technology, 1996

Bradshaw delivery van, Oxford, 2006 with postman driver Ken Beahan.
Image: Royal Mail: Courier 2006

Streamlined airmail van, Liverpool.
BPMA P599

Mobile Post Office at outdoor event in 1930s.
BPMA P2094

MPO outside
Edinburgh Castle,
Scotland.
BPMA

Amphibious vehicle.
BPMA 15017

Experimental
motor mail van
with an adapted
horse-van body,
London, 1905.
Second in a series
of postal vehicles
illustrated by
Debbie Cook.
Printed by
Harrison &
Sons Limited.

Stamp booklet, 1994.
Stamp book cover by
Debbie Cook issued in
April 1994. Number
two in a *'Postal
Vehicles'* series of
three. Depicts
experimental motor-
van adapted from a
horse-van body
operated by Mc
Namara circa 1905.
*BPMA Philatelic
collection*

The Post Office Fleet in 1959

Postal	Engineering	Road Haulage
Morris 50 cu.ft. (Z)	Morris Minor Type I	Commer 3 ton
Morris _ ton (Q)	Morris Minor Type III	Leyland 3 ton
Morris 100 cu.ft. (Y)	Morris 8cwt (Y)	Bedford 4 ton Arctic
Morris 100 cu.ft. (J)	Morris 8cwt R.I.	Commer 7 ton
Morris Cowley 100 cu.ft.	Morris 8cwt 'J'	Bedford 6 ton Arctic
Commer 100 cu.ft.	Morris Cowley 8 cwt	Hillman G.P. car
Morris 240 cu.ft	Planning vehicles	Morris 8 cwt 'Y'
Morris 240 cu.ft (F.C.)	Experimental J2	Maudslay Mogul 6 ton (H.F.)
Morris 200 cu.ft.	Morris 8cwt Utilicon	Seddon 6 ton (H.F.)
Morris 360 cu.ft.	Hillman G.P. Car	A.E.C. 8 ton ART (H.F.)
Morris 340 cu.ft.	Amphibian 'Dulw'	Foden 10 ton (H.F.)
Morris 360 cu.ft. tipper	Amphibian 'Ford'	Leyland 10 ton Hippo (H.F.)
Landrover	Hillman R.I.	Maudslay 12 ton (H.F.)
Karrier 600 cu.ft.	Hillman T.V. Detector	A.C.V. Mandator 14 ton (H.F.)
Mechanical Horse	Morris 1 ton S/C	A.E.C. Breakdown Lorry
Garage Breakdown	Appts Delivery	Forklift Truck
Mobile Post Office	Morris 1 ton 'U'	Morris Arctic 6 ton (H.F.)
Mobile Call Office	Morris 30cwt S/C	Morris 7 ton (H.F.)
Tender for Mobile Post Office	Morris 30cwt 'U'	
Morris 240 cu.ft (H.F.)	Morris 30cwt Test	**Passenger Cars**
Morris 240 cu.ft. (F.C.)	Morris 30cwt Enclosed	Standard 8 h.p.
Morris 360 cu.ft. (H.F.)	Karrier T.V.O.B.	Morris/Austin 10 h.p.
Trojan 150 cu.ft. (H.F.)	Albion 30cwt 'U'	Austin A40
Trojan 240 cu.ft. (H.F.)	Morris S.M.A.C.	Hillman 'Minx'
Seddon 250 cu.ft. (H.F.)	Karrier 25cwt Test	Morris/Wolseley 12/14 h.p.
Landrover (H.F.)	Landrover (petrol)	Morris Oxford
Morris 240 cu.ft. (H.F.)	Austin 2 ton N.F.S.	Wolseley 18 h.p.
	Karrier T-Table Ladder	Humber 'Hawk'

Telegraph	Engineering	Passenger Cars
	Leyland 3 ton S/C	Standard 'Vanguard'
Lightweight Motor Cycle (125 cc)	Albion 3 ton S/C	Humber Snipe/Pullman
(125 cc)		
Telegraph delivery vans (Z)	Albion Crane Lorry	Seddon Personnel Carrier
Telegraph delivery vans (Q)	Bedford 3 ton Q.I.	Bedford Coach (30 seat)
Mobile telegraph office	Bedford Tipper	Morris 30 cwt
	Karrier 3 ton Low Loader	Karrier 14 seat coach
Supplies Department	Bed Scammell Motive Unit	Karrier Ambulance
Morris 1 ton	Commer 4 ton S/C	
Morris 30cwt	Austin 4 ton S/C	
Albion 2-3 ton	Karrier 2 ton G/U	
Leyland 2-3 ton	Landrover Station Wagon	
Bedford 2-3 ton	Ex C&W Ford 30cwt	
Bedford 6 ton	Commer 3 _ ton	
Morris 6 ton	Ford G.P. Car	
Commer 6 ton	Fordson 3 ton	
Albion 6 ton	Fordson 2 ton	
Leyland 6 ton	Fordson Tractor	
Morris 5 cwt (Z)	Petrol Tanker	
Morris 5 cwt (Q)	Seddon 25cwt (H.F.)	
Morris Utilicon	Landrover (H.F.)	
Hillman G.P. car	Seddon 3 ton S/C (H.F.)	
Scammell M.U.	Seddon Tipper	
Seddon 25 cwt (H.F.)	Seddon Pantechnicon	
Seddon 3 ton (H.F.)	Seddon Motive Unit (H.F.)	
Morris 3 ton (H.F.)	Morris Prime Mover (H.F.)	
Morris 6 ton (H.F.)	Dennis Mobile Power Plant	
Seddon 6 ton (H.F.)	Mobile V.F. Teleg. Unit	
Morris 7 ton (H.F.)	Mobile Coastal Radio Station	
Maudslay 12 ton Major	Mobile Waveguide Workshop	
Albion 12 ton (H.F.)	Gulley Emptier	
Scammell 12 ton (H.F.)	Morris 5 ton hydraulic platform	
A.E.C. 10 ton (H.F.)	Tractor (non-track laying)	
Seddon MU	Trench Excavator	
A.E.C. Mandator MU	Mobile Crane	
Mercury (ACV)	Bulldozer	
Ransome & R 5 ton crane	International Harvester	
Forklift Truck	Fordson Tractor (H.F.)	
	Simon Hydraulic P/form	
	Forklift Truck	

British Postal Museum & Archive:
- Philatelic, object and oral history collections

The Royal Mail Archive:
Portfolio collection

POST 10	Post Office, Records of Conveyance by Road, Inland Services
POST 30	Post Office, Registered Files, Minuted Papers
POST 33	Post Office, Registered Files, Minuted Papers
POST 68	Post Office, Rules and Instructions
POST 76	Post Office, Engineering
POST 110	Post Office, Printed publicity material
POST 111	Post Office, Newspaper cuttings
POST 114	Post Office, Acts and Warrants
POST 115	Post Office, Acts and Warrants
POST 118	Post Office, Staff Association and Union Publications
POST 122	Post Office, Registered Files, Minuted and Decentralised Central Registry Papers

- Reports to the Postmaster General
- Philatelic Journal

Royal Mail Group:
- Press releases
- Royal Mail web-site
- Vehicle Services

Charles Dickens: *Little Dorrit*, pub. 1855-1857
Thomas De Quincey: *The English Mail Coach*, pub. 1849

Image Credits
All images from The Royal Mail Archive © Royal Mail Group
plc 2006
All images from The British Postal Museum & Archive collection
© The British Postal Museum & Archive 2006
Images from Royal Mail Courier and Royal Mail Vehicle Services
© Royal Mail Group plc 2006
Every reasonable effort has been taken to establish the ownership
of the images reproduced in this book and to request permission
where appropriate. Any omissions or errors are inadvertent and
will be corrected for future publication on written notification
by the rights holder or their representative.

Cover image:
Royal Mail parcel coach. Photograph c1900. *BPMA H4087*

Back cover images (clockwise from top left):
i) Poster produced by the Post Office to advertise the Telegram
   Service. Designed by Pat Keely, 1950. *BPMA P109/32 IRP 22.*
ii) One of the special Morris air mail vans, a 10cwt, 70 cubic feet
   capacity vehicle, leaving the Customs House, Croydon Airport,
   1933. *BPMA ref: P8560.*
iii) Stamp booklet, 1994 BPMA Philatelic collection. One of three
   stamp book covers by Debbie Cook issued September 1994.
   Number three in 'Postal Vehicles' series of three depicts an
   experimental electrically powered van. *BPMA Philatelic collection.*

British Postal Museum & Archive

The British Postal Museum & Archive (BPMA) holds the largest single collection of British Post Office vehicles. This collection, currently over 40 in number, reflects the diversity of the fleet and its functions.

The British Postal Museum & Archive
Freeling House
Phoenix Place
London
WC1X 0DL

Tel: 020 7239 2570
info@postalheritage.org.uk
www.postalheritage.org.uk

Post Office Vehicle Club

The Post Office Vehicle Club (POVC) was formed in 1962 by a group of people with an interest in the GPO fleet. Its members maintain an interest in the current operations and history of both Post Office (now Royal Mail Group) and BT vehicle fleets. They can be contacted via:

Frank Weston, Hon. Secretary,
Post Office Vehicle Club
32 Russell Way
Leighton Buzzard
Bedfordshire
LU7 3NG